BUSINESS EDUCATION

FOR COMPETENCE AND RESPONSIBILTY

BUSINESS EDUCATION

FOR COMPETENCE AND RESPONSIBILITY

Edited By

T H O M A S   H.   C A R R O L L

Dean, School of Business Administration
University of North Carolina

The University of North Carolina Press

CHAPEL HILL

*Manufactured in the United States of America
By the Seeman Printery, Incorporated, Durham, N. C.*

Preface

THIS VOLUME COMMEMORATES the dedication of three new buildings which serve as the home of the School of Business Administration and the Department of Economics at the University of North Carolina in Chapel Hill.

Business administration, both as a field of endeavor and as a professional area of higher education, has made substantial strides forward in the decades immediately past. Building upon past strengths and with the exercise of creative imagination and demonstration of faith in the basic principles of our American system of private enterprise, the future can be bright indeed. Academically, this may be expected to involve increased recognition of the fact that professional curricula in business administration deal with the gamut of applied social science and not with applied economics alone.

Many, if not most, professional schools of business administration have emerged from departments of economics. Thus, the historical relation between economics and business administration has obscured somewhat the full appreciation of the necessarily multiple and complicated root system of the new professional area. Certainly the disciplines of psychology, sociology, anthropology and political science, among others, have central contributions to make to the area of business administration. The relations with the discipline of economics, nevertheless, remain vitally important.

There has been a great deal of discussion recently as to whether business administration or business policy-making and execution constitutes a profession. The specific answer arrived at in such a discussion does not appear to be of crucial importance. But it is significant that business leaders—of both large and small business —have been reflecting to an increasing extent what Frank W. Abrams describes as "the hallmark of a profession," i.e., a "sense of duty" to company stockholders or owners, employees, customers and the general public alike.

James Bryant Conant, former president of Harvard University, who is now serving as our nation's High Commissioner in Germany,

has stated: ". . . . Business needs men who appreciate the responsibilities of business to itself and to that unique society of free
men which has been developed on this continent. Such men must
understand not only the practical workings of business organizations but also the economic and social climate in which business
operates. . . ." The faculty of the School of Business Administration at Chapel Hill, which includes the members of the faculty in
economics, recognizes this need. Our efforts to make a substantial
contribution toward meeting the need are reflected in all activities
of the School: (1) in its curriculum, which includes a broad and
well-balanced core of business subjects and is designed to avoid
over-specialization; (2) in its teaching—undergraduate, graduate
and executive—much of it problem-oriented, and (3) in its research
activities. Accordingly, when a dedication program was planned
we chose to invite as speakers men who, by their own actions as well
as words, have demonstrated their recognition of this broad concept
of education for responsibility.

Although Frank W. Abrams, Chairman of the Board, Standard
Oil Company (New Jersey), was unable to be present, he and the
editor of the *Harvard Business Review* acceded readily to our request that we reprint as a suitable message from him in this dedication volume his challenging article entitled "Management's Responsibilities in a Complex World." A humble and wise man, Mr.
Abrams is universally regarded as one of America's business statesmen.

Dean Donald K. David of the Harvard Graduate School of
Business Administration has had a unique combination of experience as professor, operating business executive, in service on numerous boards of directors and trustees, and for the past twelve
years as Dean of the Harvard Business School. He is looked upon
by leaders of business, business education and government as one of
America's "central figures." He is especially able to present a pene-
trating and challenging statement on the role of education for
business responsibility.

Inasmuch as many of the graduates of this School and of similar
schools enter the field of public service administration, we were
especially anxious to include a perceptive spokesman for that important segment of our society. James E. Webb, a native North

Carolinian and an alumnus of the University at Chapel Hill, appeared indeed to be an admirable choice. He has served with distinction in a number of important governmental assignments including terms of office as Director of the Bureau of the Budget of the United States and as Undersecretary of State. He is at present serving in a leadership role as an executive in private business.

Mr. George M. Harrison is looked upon by his fellow labor leaders as well as by the business executives with whom he has been in constant touch as a fair and enlightened labor leader. He seemed a natural choice for a man who could bring to the dedication program and to this volume a suitable message concerning responsibility of and to labor.

Mr. Thomas B. McCabe has served society well in a number of important roles. He is the former Chairman of the Board of Governors of the Federal Reserve System and is now President of the Scott Paper Company. Based upon his broad background of experience, he has written a message on management philosophy which emphasizes our theme of responsibility. He has also pointed out the mutual responsibility of American business and education, especially professional schools of business administration.

As I have stated elsewhere: "It is not a school or a university which accomplishes things; it is people. We must in a professional school of business administration endeavor to develop in our students the capacity to think, to produce on their jobs, to lead useful and happy lives of service. All this must be built upon sound ethical values. There is involved a real challenge to the faculty of such a professional school. We must never be completely satisfied, but we must be reasonable. We must arrive at the very difficult objective of a proper balance between education and training in a professional school. The key is constant recognition of the dynamic character of the basic problem and of the people involved."

THOMAS H. CARROLL

Chapel Hill, North Carolina
December 1953

Contents

BUSINESS EDUCATION

FOR COMPETENCE AND RESPONSIBILTY

Management's Responsibilities in a Complex World[1]

By

FRANK W. ABRAMS

Chairman of the Board, Standard Oil Company (New Jersey)

LIKE ALL VITAL, LIVING THINGS, the practice of business management is not static. It changes—sometimes at a relatively slow pace, sometimes more rapidly. I believe that a number of important changes have occurred in a comparatively brief recent period. These changes may not be widely and fully recognized. Yet they are important, not only to businessmen themselves but to all the other groups of our society who have a stake in the national economy, which means everyone.

Many businessmen, perhaps, have not been fully conscious of this evolution, simply because their day-to-day tasks keep their eyes so closely focused on their own particular part of the business picture. They do not have so much opportunity as they should to stand back and see it in its full dimensions.

Management Now a Profession

Briefly, it seems to me that business management in the United States is acquiring more and more the characteristics of a profession.

The hallmark of a profession is its sense of duty. None of the great, recognized professions is without a strong sense of responsibility to the community. Professional men do not work solely for themselves, but also for the good of mankind. The profession of medicine would not have the high standing it now enjoys if physicians did not observe the Hippocratic Oath of service. The legal profession would not be so highly regarded if it had not behind it a history of public service. The respect which the world gives to the teaching profession is not solely due to a respect for learning. It is also a salute to the men and women who have devoted themselves

[1] *Harvard Business Review*, XXIX, No. 3 (May, 1951), pp. 29-34. Published by permission of author and editor.

to one of the most important activities in society—the instruction of youth.

It is my belief that business managers are gaining in professional status partly because they see in their work the basic responsibilities that other professional men have long recognized in theirs. Businessmen are learning that they have responsibilities not just to one group but to many.

Because a large and well-established enterprise is accustomed to looking far into the future and making long-term decisions, it particularly needs broad social and political understanding as well as economic understanding.

The job of professional management, as I see it, is to conduct the affairs of the enterprise in its charge in such a way as to maintain an equitable and workable balance among the claims of the various directly interested groups. Business firms are man-made instruments of society. They can be made to achieve their greatest social usefulness—and thus their future can be best assured—when management succeeds in finding a harmonious balance among the claims of the various interested groups: the stockholders, employees, customers, and the public at large. But management's responsibility, in the broadest sense, extends beyond the search for a balance among respective claims. Management, as a good citizen, and because it cannot properly function in an acrimonious and contentious atmosphere, has the positive duty to work for peaceful relations and understanding among men—for a restoration of faith of men in each other in all walks of life.

We hear a lot about the American way of life, and the essential dignity of man. Faith in our fellow men is the only basis on which each and every one of us can live that democratic principle. Suspicion of our fellow men generally—or of any section of our fellow men because of race, economic group, or religion—is incompatible with the dignity and aspirations of men in a free society. This is a subject on which I feel keenly, and I am going to discuss it later on.

Interests of Stockholders

First, let us consider the interests of stockholders. As the owners of the business, they have invested their money in it and expect it to be run in such a way that they will receive a fair return, security, and a reasonable gain in the value of their equity as the industry grows.

Those two words, "fair" and "reasonable," mark the asserted claims not only of a corporation's stockholders but of all other groups as well. Very few groups ever believe that they make unfair or unreasonable claims. But often what one group thinks fair is regarded as entirely unreasonable by another. It takes professional judgment, experience, and knowledge of the consequences of specific decisions to resolve all the claims and to keep all the groups in cooperative support of the joint enterprise.

This reconciliation of interests is not always as difficult as it may seem. It is in part a matter of recognizing true long-term interests, as distinguished from interests that may seem real because they are more immediate.

There was a time, not so very long ago, when management thought of itself as being exclusively preoccupied with the stockholders' *immediate* interest. The stockholder, who had invested his capital in the enterprise, naturally had an interest in maximizing profits and dividends. As a general rule, therefore, management, as the stockholders' representative, vigorously contested the claims of labor for higher wages, and of customers for lower prices and better quality unless competition decreed otherwise. In that way higher profits and dividends, it was believed, could best be realized.

Let us examine that notion more closely to see whether such an attitude was really in the interest of the stockholder. It might have been if the stockholder was an in-and-out speculator. But if he was an investor, and had committed his capital for the purpose of acquiring an equity in a continuing enterprise that might grow and prosper over the years, then his interest might have been very badly served by such an attitude on the part of his management representatives.

Public approval is no less essential to the continued existence of today's kind of business than adequate capital, or efficient management. A satisfied and loyal group of employees, for instance, is an asset to the enterprise and its owners, of far greater value for its long-term success than many other items which carry a dollar-and-cents valuation in the balance sheet.

The Nature of Profits. Even profits, it has come to be realized, are not so much an immediate prerogative of stockholders as was once thought. True, in the accounting sense and in the legal sense, all profits accrue to the beneficial interest of shareholders, but that does not necessarily mean that shareholders receive in payment all of what is accounted as profits.

If management is to make good its responsibility to preserve the long-run interests of stockholders, it must produce job opportunities in which men can maximize their productivity. That takes money. The task is an impossible one without the availability of adequate profits, a large part of which are directly or indirectly reinvested.

It can thus be seen that profits are not simply a withdrawal from the business for the exclusive benefit of stockholders. Actually they are used in large part to make secure the competitive position of the enterprise by increasing the productivity of its workers and thus, as an all important by-product, increasing the real income of the nation.

Only by thinking of profits in these larger terms can management feel assured that it is doing an effective job in the stockholders' over-all interest. Fortunately, in the long run, the stockholders' interest and the other interests of the community tend to coincide, and enlightened stockholders are seeing this more clearly all the time.

Management and Employees

Just as stockholders have invested their money, so, too, the men and women who work for a corporation have invested their time, their energies, and many of their hopes for security and happiness in their jobs. The employee's satisfaction comes not only from fair wages but from good working conditions—and also from opportunities for promotion and recognition as the business grows. But this is not all.

"The dignity of man"—the deep-seated desire to be treated like a worthy human being—has long been a foundation stone of our way of life. The claim of all employees to respect and consideration as human beings, with ambition and the capacity for self-improvement, poses a major responsibility for the management of any modern business. In fact, modern business management might well measure its success or failure as a profession in large part by the satisfaction and opportunities it is able to produce for its employees.

In the modern corporation the worker is no longer Check Number 273 of some department. He is John Wesley Jones or Michael Doroski. His satisfactions and his contribution to the success of the enterprise will be directly proportional to his understanding of the part he plays in its accomplishments, and to the opportunity that he has to participate and take pride in its progress.

In one of our affiliated companies, some years ago, there was a case of dissatisfaction among a group of workers. We knew the dissatisfaction existed, but we could not find out why. The management discussed many things with this group, including wages, and did not come anywhere near solving the problem. But some time later the president of that company was talking things over with the men and began to mention, in an informal way, some of the matters the board of directors had been dealing with. The men showed an immediate and extraordinary interest, and the source of their dissatisfaction was gradually revealed. They had been "left out of things." Needless to say, that situation was changed, and we are continually applying ourselves to means for keeping employees better informed.

In stressing the modern corporation's responsibilities to its employees, I am not advocating a program of paternalism. Businesses are in business to make money and not to stand in the place of parents, school, or church. But what I am saying is that no corporation can prosper for any length of time today if its sole purpose is to make as much money as possible, as quickly as possible, and without concern for other values. A modern corporation management, which has developed good social sense as well as good business sense, will accept the major responsibility to contribute to a satisfactory way of life for the men and women who work for it.

Management and the Customers

The customers make up a third group which has claims on business management. As any corporate manager knows, customers are in the driver's seat. They are very likely to demand and gain pretty much what they want. A large part of the skill and technique of management is devoted to the professional task of co-ordinating and synchronizing the capital of stockholders with the talents of workers in a manner that will most effectively give the customer what he wants—more and better products at reasonable prices.

It has long been accepted that large volumes at small margins —preferably with gradually declining prices—is a formula that has contributed to the success of American enterprise. Practice has not always conformed to the formula, but it has done so reasonably well. Competition has assured that result in American industry. But I think that in these times of great demands upon business and industry, and of threats to all freedom including economic freedom, it is appropriate to reaffirm our belief in competition and rededicate ourselves to practices that will aid in making it effective.

The oil industry offers many illustrations of providing better products at reasonable prices. For example, the average retail price of gasoline received by the vendor is about the same today as it was 25 years ago. Of course, that does not include the taxes paid on it by the consumer, which have increased more than threefold since then.

Furthermore, since the quality of gasoline has steadily improved in the last quarter of a century, the power delivered by two gallons of today's gasoline is equal to three gallons of 1925 motor fuel. While costs have materially advanced, the price of gasoline—less taxes—is about the same as it was although the quality is much better.

That is what I mean when I say that it is a responsibility of modern professional management to recognize the long-term claims of its customers to a better and better buy when they go to the market place for products. That is the way that the unprecedented achievements of American industry have been accomplished, and we must not for an instant lose sight of that principle.

During the last 50 years, especially, there have been times when the pressure on prices to advance or to contract violently has been great. Although many of the forces that make for inflation or deflation are outside the control of businessmen, I firmly believe that management, in the exercise of true business statesmanship, should do all in its power to dampen disruptive swings in the behavior of prices. Great instability is not in the interest of the stockholders or the employees—and it is certainly not in the interest of the customers.

Business management *does* have a responsibility to provide a flow of supplies needed to meet the requirements of the economy. Therefore, I believe, we must always try to foresee the results of a particular price change in terms of its effect on probable future supplies. It would be hard to show that the public interest is served by price changes that do not assist in stimulating either supply or demand, as one or the other may be needed from time to time.

Now these three groups that I have considered are the people with whom corporation managements have a direct and working contact. They are all very important. Each of their interests must be served and related one to the other, to the best of management's ability.

The General Public's Interest

But that is not the end of the story—the general public has a vital interest as well. Modern management must look beyond those groups of people that are immediately interested in the affairs of the business. It must understand that the general public—men and women everywhere—have a very deep interest in, and are affected by, what is going on. Contemporary management realizes that the actions it takes have definite and often far-reaching effects—effects that go beyond stockholders, employees, and customer.

The duty of business management to the general public is of a twofold nature. First, there is the obligation to keep the policies and actions of a particular business constantly in tune with national policies and interests, because in many cases a company is a very large factor in a community.

The second phase of this obligation to attend to the public interest arises out of the fact that the thing we call public interest is crystallized in public policy, and public policy has a very positive ultimate bearing on the success of the businesses that are entrusted to our care. We must participate in the formation of public policy even though the specific issues may not have an immediate influence on our individual businesses. Business historians will tell you that there was a time when businessmen shared the intellectual leadership of society with educators and churchmen. In recent decades the opportunity for intellectual leadership at times seems to have become confused with the urge to compete with other minority groups in special-interest pleading.

Participation in Public Attitudes

Business management cannot afford that indulgence. The geographical pioneering of this country's development is pretty much accomplished. Population has increased and shifted to the point where congestion occurs in many locations. The problems incident to increased population are accentuated by more rapid transportation and improved means of communication. People have been brought into closer association. Their opportunities for personal differences have multiplied.

It has become more important for us to learn how to live in harmony in a new kind of world. People now are more concerned with each other, and much less with the mastery of their physical environment. The importance of faith in our fellow men, and understanding among men, is thereby made the greater. Yet suspicion and acrimony exist among people and seem to be growing stronger. In words that have been attributed to Dean McIntosh of Barnard, "While man has brought his physical universe under control, he cannot manage the simple relations between himself and his fellows."

Well, then, what can be done about it? In my opinion, there is one thing that can be done, and that is to spend a lot more of our thought and our energies as business managers in working to achieve a redistribution of faith, and less in what has come to be a somewhat sterile discussion of redistribution of wealth.

Management must apply to its relationships with the rest of the community the same type of searching analysis that it would make of its more usual business problems. It must do this in terms of what it knows, and can learn, about the basic wants and needs of men. After all, when you stop to think about it, it is absurd that business and the public, of which business is a part, should be regarded as being in conflict; or, again, that management should be opposed to labor's basic interest, and labor to management's.

All this may sound pretty idealistic. It is. But it also can be very practical. Trust among people can be recaptured only if we succeed in breaking through the *separatism* that has grown up among groups. We must aim to tear down the psychological walls that have been built around group interests. We must realize that in these matters the whole is greater than the sum of its parts. Business management must make its own contribution to a restoration of understanding and faith among men.

The American Tradition of Self-Examination. To be certain that we make our full contribution to the welfare of all, we businessmen must recognize the possibility that we may have become possessed of some of those suspicions and fears that are so clear to us when we see them in others. We too may have lost some of our faith in our fellow men. What can we of good faith in the business community do about minimizing suspicions among the dominant groups of the country, including ourselves? We can make a brave start by examining the area about which we should know the most—ourselves.

Management can make sure that any action it takes or sponsors in its own behalf is clearly justified, in the light of principle. At all costs, it should avoid building bear traps for business. Conscientious care and restraint must guide us in anything that touches us personally, such as our own compensation. We must curb our occasional enthusiams for special government protection or other forms of assistance. We must be sure we do not support the imposition of measures within the economy that are beneficial only to the interests that we may personally represent—measures that may fail to serve the interests, or may even be contrary to the interests, of everyone else.

But self-discipline and restraint by business management, essential though they are, are not enough if we are to succeed in re-establishing genuine public acceptance of our economic leadership. We must re-establish the common touch with our fellow men. We must reappear in the role of warmhearted human beings—which is what we are.

It always amazes me when I consider how many of the leaders of business and industry today have come from very humble circumstances. Most of the people I know in high positions not only were born barefooted, but many of them stayed that way for some time.

But it is true—and I think we can see it everywhere—that as success comes and men rise to positions of responsibility, they start going to the same clubs, talking to each other, playing golf in the same foursomes, making speeches to each other, and generally building up a wall around themselves. Perhaps our business leadership needs to go back to school to relearn the art of knowing all the people. Of course one may point to exceptions; I know there are many. But there is plenty of truth in the picture, too.

Selling Ourselves Personally. What I am trying to say is that I do not think that business has a chance to do the kind of job it honestly wants to do, and the kind of job for which it is trained and equipped—it does not have a chance to make its full contribution to the welfare of all—unless businessmen get out and sell themselves personally to the other major groups that make up the people of good faith in America. Part of that selling is the exercise of conscientious care and restraint in our businesses and part is the simple matter of remeeting the "folks." I am sure that too few people really know those responsible in business organizations. We have gone too far down the road of setting up what might be called a business aristocracy, simply by mingling and talking only with ourselves.

It is easy to be suspicious of the aims and purposes of people you do not know. The foundation of good human relationships must be faith, and it is hard to have faith in a strange name on a piece of paper. We frequently feel hurt that our motives are questioned and our sincerity doubted. But all the advertising space we can buy, exhorting others to believe in us as businessmen, will go unheeded, and all our speeches and statements will fall on deaf ears, until folks believe that we understand and are concerned with their problems.

The business leaders of this nation are able, intelligent, and informed men. They have a responsibility to the nation, as well as to their businesses, to re-establish themselves in the public mind as objective thinkers and seekers of the public interest. It is entirely proper that they should do this, because in the long run the public interest corresponds with the basic interests of their individual businesses.

Business managers must merit the confidence of the nation, so that they can more effectively contribute to the solution of the many complex social questions of our time. Unless this reservoir of intelligence and capacity for action can be made available to the solution of some of these social problems, I cannot have great confidence that satisfactory solutions will be found. There is no higher responsibility, there is no higher duty, of professional management than to gain the respect of the general public through objective participation in, and consideration of, national questions, even though these questions in many cases do not relate directly to their immediate business problems.

Attitudes and Practices in Transition

We must not be impatient. Business attitudes and practices change, but they sometimes change slowly. Looking back on that uncharted period when American business was growing to maturity, we may be inclined to feel that some of those early businessmen neglected their social responsibilities. But we must not forget that it was a time of pioneering when a sense of corporate responsibility in terms of present-day standards had not yet developed. In fact, the need was not even recognized.

My business experience goes back more than 38 years with the Standard Oil Company (New Jersey). This service spans an important period in the industrial development of our country and in the shaping of new philosophies to guide management. Management has grown enormously in the understanding of its responsibilities. It has become not only the promoter of the prosperity of the enterprise but a participant in the adjustment of the claims of the several groups that I have mentioned. Regardless of our consciousness of the Bible directive, the machine age in which we live has, in a sense, caused all of us to become our brothers' keepers. We must recapture and hold to faith in each other.

There is an underlying patriotic motive in all of this which an intelligent management thoroughly understands. In a democratic state, only those institutions which so conduct themselves as to deserve, secure, and hold public confidence can survive and prosper.

It is a plain ordinary fact that our country, to be strong and constructive in a troubled world, is dependent upon free, competitive institutions to give its people opportunity of self-expression and advancement. If we are to be helpful in advancing our American way of life, we must be willing to show by example that individual objectives can best be served when they are identified with the common good.

And the serving of individual objectives by identifying them with the common good, I firmly believe, will lead to the increasing recognition of business management as a profession—for such service is the essence of a profession.

The Tasks of Business Education

Dean, Harvard Graduate School of Business Administration

THE DEDICATION OF THESE BUILDINGS offers opportunity for renewed dedication to the goals of education. I bring with me Harvard's congratulations and good wishes upon North Carolina's acquisition of these essential facilities. But more important even than the beauty and utility of these buildings is the opportunity for education which they symbolize. I should like to deal with the need and opportunity for business education—especially here in a place where promise is bright and at a moment when attention is focused upon it. If the School of Business Administration here at Chapel Hill, like ours and those of other universities, is to meet the needs in business, labor, and government, it must accept a difficult mission. The demand for creative leadership in these areas is great; the need for it in education itself is therefore urgent.

The role of the business schools has changed rapidly in the half century of their existence—in the direction of increased usefulness, expanded purpose, and wider acceptance. Time *was* (and perhaps in some quarters time still *is*) when most commerce or business schools were narrowly oriented toward partial mastery of vocational techniques. As the University schools groped through their early years, they were often greeted by much criticism—deserved or not—from older disciplines. The relationship of economics departments to business schools was a persistent problem; the conflicting aims of liberal and vocational education divided faculties; relationships with business were not always easily established; budgetary limitations prevented a "breakout" from other problems; and the usefulness of education for business in *school* as opposed to actual *work* experience was not easy to demonstrate.

These problems have not all been solved, but they have been tackled. Dealing with persistent problems is usually a maturing experience. Through the years of relatively slow acceptance, our business schools have matured. They have significantly improved their claim for respect in academic, business, and government circles. They have made much progress in establishing standards by which curricula can be judged and schools accredited. Their product has been sought *by* business and government and has typically proved successful *in* business and government.

It is believed that this fortunate outcome is traceable to a change of focus away from vocational techniques toward a slowly broadening concept of administration. I mean by "administration" the accomplishment of the proper purposes of an organization by, through, and with people. The current concept of administration has unified the study of accounting, finance, marketing and production and has given recognizable shape to business education. The enormous range of disease prevention and cure in medicine (to look at an older profession) centers upon maintenance of health and healing the sick. The enormous range of business activity now seems to cluster about leadership in work in an association of individuals brought together for a common purpose.

It is now the immediate responsibility of the business schools to provide business with able men equipped to learn well from experience how to become administrators. With the shortage of executive skills, the need to reconcile divergent activities of technical specialists, the new emphasis on human and social responsibilities, and the increasingly tough demands of hard competition, management needs our help. Business needs our trained young men, our advanced training for experienced specialists, and our cooperation in company training programs. The emphasis on administration has brought many of our schools beyond the vocational purposes which begot them. It has crystallized the contribution of business education to business.

As our schools have matured in the training of men for business, they have caught sight of a professional, rather than a vocational, objective. The idea of professional competence has come to include a sense of responsibility for the impact of individual business activity upon our whole economic system and upon our society of free men using material plenty as the means to a full life. Essentially, our business education has broadened its horizons even faster than it has gathered information, explored new fields, and developed courses. As it has grown in activity and purpose, it has tended closer and closer in spirit to the basic aims of a liberal education. The better business schools have enormous distances yet to go, but the distance already traveled in a very short time is impressive, given the rate and nature of change in most academic institutions.

The task of business education henceforth is essentially the communication of professional attitudes and abilities. Our schools each have opportunity for creative leadership in education, first, in improving the method of communication and, second, in the development of new leadership and concepts to communicate.

To this end, we at the Harvard Business School have long been interested in the educational process itself. We are aware, of course, of how little is known and how much there is to be known about learning. This awareness pervades all educational institutions, but in business schools it is acute. The maturing of business education now includes the recognition that the acquisition of knowledge and information—to be remembered or forgotten—is not the main goal so much as the development of judgment, of ways of thinking, of points of view, and effective patterns of action. Professional attitudes, for example, are not easy to teach. The medical and the teaching fraternities conduct themselves like professions and their professional attitudes are communicated as powerful social codes. Business is not yet always conducted or regarded as a profession. Business schools thus must learn how to originate or at least invoke and develop professional values and aspirations in their students, how to convey the truth that in the practice of administration one can find the high and permanent satisfactions common to all the professions. How to teach becomes, therefore, a matter of urgent inquiry rather than of assumption. Business schools have opportunity not only to improve the methods by which they make learning possible for their students but also to influence business in the same direction. Research into the learning process, with the classroom and the living hall as the laboratory, is needed to increase our knowledge of the educational activity we superintend.

Essential also to supplying the needs for leadership in the organizations for which we train men and women is the selection of basically sound candidates for degrees. To supply the almost limitless demands for leadership, we must attract to administration a group of able men who go into business not after eliminating other possibilities but as first choice. To accomplish this purpose, change must take place in the attitudes toward business which students learn during the course of their training in the liberal arts and in their earlier education. It is gratifying to note at long last that professors in economics, history, and literature are reexamining their attitudes toward business administration as a career.

But even more vitally important than research into learning and the assembly of a fine student body is the development of a business faculty. Good teaching is essential in the educational process. The teacher's own awareness of the goals of business education, his own knowledge of administration and his own values will determine how deeply his students are encouraged to inquire, how much they learn, and how completely they subscribe to professional principles of service and competence. The greatest opportunity for school administrators is providing as best they can the conditions under which a self-governing body of scholars continually increases in caliber and in knowledge of what their calling requires them to know. The best schools have the best faculties.

I should like to turn from the problems of communicating what is presently perceived to the formation of new knowledge and the achievement of new insight. The growth of business schools has been accompanied by significant achievements. By way of new knowledge, a literature has sprung up to record much of what is now known in all the business fields. Experimental research has been limited, but surveys have been initiated and continued and a body of statistical data has been accumulated. Even more significantly for administrators, the assembly of thousands of clinical situations from businesses has given us teaching materials and enables us to formulate working hypotheses and methods of observation.

By way of new insight made possible by this new knowledge, we have enlarged the concept of the administrator. We have merged the ideals of *competence* and *responsibility*. At the Harvard Business School (to make no claims but to refer to what I know best), we have learned as a result of research into human relations in industry and of inquiry into relationships between our economy, our government, and our whole society, that the aspiring executive must perceive that leadership in getting the world's work done by, through, and with people is a high calling. Preparation for becoming and remaining an effective administrator now includes a willingness to consider and provide for the non-economic needs of individuals within their organizations, to provide not only a livelihood but a satisfying way of life, to furnish the opportunity for individual growth and to make available at work more of the same kind of satisfactions a free citizen finds elsewhere in his life.

What still needs doing surpasses what has been done. We need first much more study of the traditional fields of business. We are not finished there, for methods in marketing, manufacturing, control and finance continually change in directions that must be foreseen, recorded, or pointed out by the schools. The newest field, human relations, is still in its infancy; the alteration and extension of studies in other fields made possible by the findings here are still largely unexplored. No course, in even the traditional fields can long remain the same, for new developments and new combinations of knowledge compel continuous change—never for its own sake but always for advancement. We need more research into the workings of competition, the influence of big business and big labor, the achievement of stabilized employment and increasing productivity —the place of business in our industrial civilization and in the world—to name only a few familiar subjects.

We need more and better clinical data. The "clinical method" of observing and recording situations confronting administrators in particular organizations must, I think, be a continuous activity of leading business schools. A faculty and a school must, of course, be generally familiar with what is going on. Its teaching must reflect current, rather than historic, reality. But even more important, the training of administrators, research workers, and faculty is incomplete without the actual experience of trying to discern relationships, isolate problems, determine factors relevant to decisions, and trying to reach decisions that have to be made by a person in a position of responsibility every day.

Observation of current situations in industry, detection of the uniformities in them, and familiarity with current practice constitute the only sound basis for developing hypotheses to guide the future research which will expand further the horizons of business knowledge. We do not maintain contact with current business practice merely to know it, but to analyze it for adequacy, to contribute to it, and to improve it where it needs improvement. The elaboration of theory without reference to the reality which theory is supposed to explain, to render predictable, or to guide comes (as all too often in economics, for example) to very little. Life, it is assumed, is a proper objective for theory. Constant reference to it is, like reflection upon it and sufficient detachment from it, indispensable to realistic guides for new research. A school must run ahead of practice and teach for the future. This necessity, it has been observed, produces impatience and sometimes temporary frustration in its graduates, but these in themselves are incentives to progress in practice.

Further study of the business functions by means of clinical observations in business organization will thus make possible fruitful new research. This we need, as Dean Thomas H. Carroll of Chapel Hill has said, to effect convergence of theory and practice. New findings will extend the leadership of the school over current practice, may complete the professionalization of management training, and may help us define further the nature of what we call the administrative process. It will help us recognize and help fill the needs of labor, management and government.

Business itself has accepted research as a concept and maintains laboratories for product development and new technical knowledge. Business will also join in research in administration as it recognizes the opportunities to support the inquiry which must now, like technical research years ago, be initiated by the universities. Through such cooperation as that provided for in the establishment of the Business Foundation of North Carolina, new research will go forward, provided that schools define important projects which need support and promise illuminating results.

To be most useful this new research should not result in further specialization. We do not need new facts so much as new combinations. We do not feel the need of more information, but of more insight useful to the performance of professional tasks. I expect and hope that the business schools taking advantage of the opportunity for leadership in education will be those which derive new concepts from previously uncombined researches.

A profession, unlike a highly specialized discipline, depends for new ideas not only upon the clinical examination of actual situations but also upon the work of scholars in many other fields. To extend the analogy between medicine and administration, referred to previously, it is revealing that our medical schools have adapted to the profession of medicine previously unrelated discoveries in biology, chemistry, physics and psychology. Electricity, bacteriology and botany do not seem far apart when they are made to serve particular problems in medical diagnosis and therapy.

Research in business administration has begun, but has not yet proceeded far in, the combination for professional practice of the sweep of scholarship in a number of special fields. To cite once again an example from experience at the Harvard Business School, Wallace B. Donham, L. J. Henderson, and Elton Mayo, themselves of diverse backgrounds, put together their knowledge of business, sociology, psychology and anthropology to produce human relations, now recognized as a valid area of research and a major field of study. These men had a rare gift for combination and application which we need to encourage in ourselves and others.

We must move forward, in particular, with the social sciences. A business school should not, I believe, consider itself solely an institution of applied economics, but the gap between business and economics should be closed by the development of an economic theory which is recognizably usable as an account of and guide to business activity. This is not the duty of the business school alone, but of students of social science as well. We need new applications of findings developed by political scientists and scholars of the law. This adaptation is not easy, for knowledge in the social sciences is not as easy to draw upon as in the exact sciences; the professional requirement is that adaptable combinations must be achieved. The relationship of the medical schools to the physical and biological sciences may eventually be paralleled by the relationship of the fully matured business school to the social sciences.

If we will put to professional use the achievements of the social sciences, we will thereby indirectly encourage useful inquiry by others. Developing concepts of administration should also involve an investigation of the achievements of the humanities—history, literature, religion, music and art. These disciplines contribute to the development of individuals worthy of professional responsibility. If administration is ever to be generally considered a profession, administrators must have the breadth of view, the sense of values, and the knowledge of life's meanings which should be made available by study of the humanities. Although limited time is involved, as in your undergraduate school, for both a liberal and a professional program, the need for a liberal education is no less great. Here are implications for *both* liberal arts and business faculties. On the one hand the liberal arts faculty may wish to examine the suitability for professional preparation of the studies it offers and on the other the business faculty must continue to acknowledge the need of its students for such training. Since school is only the beginning of an education in any case, the need for further self-education in the arts as in business needs continued emphasis.

Those responsible for new concepts and combinations in business also need the knowledge made available by scholarship in fields of the humanities. Knowledge of the goals of our own society, the forces at work in international relations, the conflict of cultures, are indispensable to the scholar of business. The highly esoteric product of scholarship is of little value, but the permanent achievement of humane studies is relevant to the study of administration—professionally defined. Business itself recognizes and emphasizes the importance and the relevance of liberal arts education in its current corporate support of liberal arts colleges.

What has been stated above underlines the breadth of *our* opportunity for creative leadership in the field of business education. It is hoped that all of us in education will set out to strengthen the relationships among the departmentalized divisions of our universities, on the one hand, and the relationships between our schools and business itself, on the other. As we reach out for the tasks described and achieve some competence in accomplishing them, the future growth of business education, enveloping and moving beyond our present problems, appears quite clear. We can and we will attract to our schools the students and the faculty who will be equal to what is demanded of them by management, by labor, by government, and by the public at large. We will attract increased financial support as our contributions to business and to society become more conspicuous. We will achieve greater cooperation of older disciplines as the essential unity of purpose, which the professional character of administration is beginning to make clear, comes home to them.

It is my hope that your school will continue its splendid progress toward accomplishing the tasks upon which I have touched. I trust that your faculty will continue its progress in the teaching of what is known and the discovery of important new concepts to teach. Inspiration and renewed enthusiasm undoubtedly will be derived from these beautiful buildings. The potentialities for accomplishment made possible here are many and you have every good wish for success in realizing them.

Responsibility in Our Free Economy

GEORGE M. HARRISON

Grand President, Brotherhood of Railway Clerks
and Vice-President, American Federation of Labor

IT IS A PLEASURE, indeed, to be privileged to participate in this program to dedicate the new buildings of the School of Business Administration of the University of North Carolina. I congratulate the University on this splendid program of expansion and development and extend good wishes for continuing progress.

It is well that our universities are so keenly aware of their increasing responsibility to the nation. Expanding population, coupled with an expanding economy, requires the expansion of the plan of our educational institutions to meet the increasing need for trained minds in all fields of thought and human endeavor. No American university has a better reputation, both for improving its facilities and for modernizing its public attitudes, than this great North Carolina institution.

The trade union movement of the United States has had an ever-growing interest in the educational system of our country. For over a century, the trade unions have been among the foremost proponents of expanding the educational opportunities of our whole population and of free, compulsory universal education. Since those early beginnings, the principle of free education for all has received such wide acceptance that it is now taken for granted by all segments of the population and in all areas of the nation. The trade union movement is proud of the part it has had in this development.

Free, compulsory universal education has served as the principal stone in the foundation upon which the great industrial and cultural developments of our nation have been built. Modern industry, like our democratic institutions, requires literate people. Freedom for the individual, without which there can be no human dignity, depends upon at least a minimum education of every individual.

Universal general education, however, meets only part of our needs. One of the strengths of our nation has been the readiness of our institutions of higher learning to adapt themselves to the demands of our society for specially trained minds. Thus we have seen developments of agricultural colleges which have done so much in our country to bring scientific methods to bear upon the problems of food supply. Men trained in these colleges have examined in all its facets the problem of tilling the soil: land utilization, soil content, seed selection, plant breeding and pest control. Similar study has been made of animal husbandry. The result in both fields has been a revolution in agricultural methods. Our land has blossomed and brought forth in our century for the first time in the history of mankind a food supply far greater than the needs of our people. The benefits of scientific methods in the United States hold the promise that the problem of food supply in the world can be solved and that famine and hunger can be wiped from the face of the globe.

We have had a similar development in industry. Our institutions of higher learning have kept pace with the demands of industry through the establishment of engineering colleges and institutes of technology. Scientific methods developed in these schools have been in turn productive of great results in industry. New products which contribute to the well-being of our people are daily being announced by industrial research specialists.

But here it is well to sound a note of caution. It is in the field of production of these items where the results have been most amazing. We must always remember that the end purpose of industry is human satisfaction, human development. The battle is only half won when our scientists and inventors have discovered or devised a product that will contribute to that end. It remains for the trained minds of management of industry to devise the methods whereby the product can be produced at a cost low enough to place it within the reach of our people generally. Availability to the people of the products of industry becomes the measure by which industrial management must be judged. There is little doubt, on measuring the management of our industry by this test, that they have very largely succeeded. This is true despite the fact that there are still arid groups in our population to whom the products of our industry do not flow in amounts sufficient to maintain a decent standard of living.

Thus, there is no doubt that the trained minds of American scientists and American management of industry have solved the problems of the production of goods for human needs. This solution applies not only to our country; the application of these methods is just as valid in other parts of the world as in America. So far as technical knowledge is concerned, there is no longer any necessity for anyone to be poorly clad or hungry. Man, by the application of his own powers, can produce enough to provide a high standard of comfort and well-being for himself. But, in the face of all this knowledge, there still remains one mystery, one great unsolved problem—how can we distribute the products of industry so that all persons shall enjoy a living standard of health and decency.

Those branches of science engaged with the problems of production of wealth and the management of industry will continue to discover in the years to come still more efficient methods of producing goods for human consumption. The increasing emphasis being placed upon the problems of distribution of those goods will undoubtedly result in methods that will bring wider and wider numbers of persons into the enjoyment of a healthy and decent standard of life. The solution of this problem of distribution is the challenge of the second half of the 20th century; an increased emphasis must be given to its study. It is in this field, too, that we must look to the universities for leadership. From our universities we must not ask the solution of this problem; rather, we should request that the attention of the minds of the thousands of persons who come to their hallowed halls for training be directed toward the problem.

The problems of production have been solved by free men. Undoubtedly these free minds applied to the problems of society—free management, free research, free agriculture, free consumers and free labor—have each made a great contribution. Freedom for all these groups can be preserved, while at the same time we seek a solution for the problems of distribution. That solution will be found sooner under our free institutions than it possibly could under any authoritarian, autocratic system.

But we must not be complacent in the face of this problem. Our economic system throughout its history has been afflicted with periodic crises and, at the present time, many economists are again raising the storm signals. Idle men, idle machines and unused raw materials all present at the same time and place in the face of unfilled needs of the people, do not make sense to men endowed with reason. If we are to maintain our free economy, the solution must come from the stewards of our free economy. If they fail, the people will demand a solution from their government. The stewards of society charged with the direction of finance, industry, labor, agriculture and our educational institutions are obligated to bring to this problem minds dedicated to human freedom and progress.

Democracy needs strong leadership in all the fields of endeavor, but strong leadership alone is no guarantee that democracy will be preserved. The freedom they enjoy in leadership must be tempered by a sense of responsibility—not narrowly in relation only to their own immediate problems, but broadly in relation to the nation as a whole. Powerful economic groups frequently take action which adversely affects the general welfare. It is at these points of action, especially, where we need strong leadership with dedicated minds fully conscious of the effect of their actions on all areas of the economy and all segments of society.

Our colleges of engineering and our colleges of business administration are supplying the trained men to manage industry which our complex society requires. Those educational institutions must also insure the dedication of the minds they are training. Our constantly improving mass production methods make it increasingly necessary that those management representatives responsible for the programming of production and the application of personnel policies have a human approach to, as well as scientific understanding of, the human problems involved in managing large labor forces. All too frequently our contacts with university trained representatives of industry in management, supervision and technical positions have disclosed a great lack of understanding of this human problem in industry. It is here that the schools of business administration can be most effective.

The counterpart of free management is free labor—free to organize in trade unions, to resist the temptation of management to try shortcuts of centralized authoritarian controls. Much is already being done in the colleges of business administration in this field of human relations. There is room for much more to be done. The personnel department of many large corporations is without status and exercises little influence upon the determination of larger management policies. Personnel managers are seemingly the scapegoat of management—someone to blame when conflagrations break out, rather than, as they should be, the instruments of management to avoid the striking of the fatal spark. So long as our schools of business administration graduate future business managers of that mentality, they are failing in their obligation to our society.

It is no secret that one of the chief problems for many American industries is the development of skills and understanding to deal with organized labor. Workers of today comprehend the great potential of American industry, business and finance. They are, therefore, insistent that our economy continue to provide in the future, as it has in the past, an ever rising standard of living for the people. Today's worker believes, and justly so, that he is entitled to share equitably in the improved joint output of capital, management and labor. Unless an equitable share of the increased productivity of industry goes to the workers, there can be no solution for the problems of distribution. Economic crises will continue to recur periodically, and the needs of the people will go unsatisfied while men and machines are idle.

It may be suggested that one of the reasons for this lack of understanding of the worker in industry is that too many of our present leaders of industry do not appreciate the important role which the organized labor movement plays in the daily lives of their employees. Therefore, it is important that the young men and women attending this school who are the potential leaders of tomorrow, should be given an objective presentation of the great contribution which American trade unions have made and are continuing to make in the development of and the preservation and extension of democracy in this country and throughout the world. The curriculum should contain not only such obvious courses as labor history, organizational structure and philosophy of labor, and labor legislation, but should also include a study of the increasingly decisive role which American labor is playing in world affairs, and of its uncompromising hostility to every brand of totalitarianism—whether it be Communism, Fascism, Nazism, Falangism, Peronism, or just plain military dictatorship.

Now, may I turn to a more direct type of relationship between the university and the organizations of labor, a relationship considered to be of special significance in the South. Among the many interesting developments in our dynamic economy is the gradual transition of the southern states from an agricultural to an industrial economy. This industrial revolution is well advanced in the great State of North Carolina. Objective students of this development expect that increasing numbers of industrial workers will join unions during the next few years. The administrative officers and faculty of this great university are no doubt giving serious consideration to educational services they can provide this growing trade union movement—particularly in the field of training responsible labor leaders.

The American labor movement has been pleased at the growing recognition on the part of institutions of higher learning of their responsibility for developing labor education programs in cooperation with trade unions. Perhaps the best known of these labor leadership training programs is the intensive thirteen-week resident course for union representatives held annually since 1942 at the Harvard Graduate School of Business Administration. The purpose of this course is to provide training for executive responsibility and to help union officers play more useful roles in the labor movement. It extends to trade unions the same basic type of training for administrative responsibility which Harvard University has long offered for men in the public civil service and men entering business administration.

Many universities are now offering their educational services to unions through their extension divisions. Courses are held in union halls in such subjects as shop steward training, collective bargaining techniques, job evaluation, time and motion study, labor legislation, and grievance procedure. Because American labor unions recognize the importance of training their leaders and members, they finance and conduct educational programs of their own in addition to the many fine programs offered by institutions of higher learning. Today, most of our large unions have established Departments of Education staffed with professionally trained teachers who conduct a wide variety of educational programs, using the most modern audio-visual techniques. These programs run the complete gamut—from classes for top leadership down through the lower echelon to classes for new members.

I am confident that the University of North Carolina will receive the hearty and enthusiastic cooperation of southern labor leaders in planning a well-balanced labor education program which should ultimately result in sound and peaceful industrial relations in this great state.

The degree to which the economy of the South moves forward in the years ahead depends in large measure upon the degree of statesmanship, cooperation and mutual goodwill displayed by the leaders of industry, labor and education in working toward common goals. General Dwight D. Eisenhower, in his inaugural address as President of Columbia University, pointed up the need for business, labor and educational leaders working closely together. He said, "The school that enjoys a partnership with manufacturing industries and labor unions and mercantile establishments of its community is a better and more productive school in consequence of its non-academic associations. Its influence permeates the entire community and is multiplied many times over while the school itself, energized by the challenges and dynamism of community life, grows and broadens with each problem it helps surmount."

The University of North Carolina seeks, and largely succeeds in its effort, to be of service to the whole community. Just as colleges must draw upon all parts of the community to build well-rounded programs, so students in our colleges must develop minds that comprehend the effect of their decisions upon all parts of our economic machinery. Unless they realize that an equitable balance must be kept between the interest of consumers, farmers, employers and laborers, our economic machinery will continue to come to periodic halts.

The wage-price-profit relationship of a single company has far wider effect than merely upon the stockholders and work force of that company. The tax policy of our governments, so largely influenced by the leaders of industry, has a profound effect upon the economy and the resulting socially desirable achievements. Increasingly, too, many vital services to farmers, to business, to labor can be rendered only by government assistance. It would be not only good social policy, but good business economics as well, to have the students of business understand these facts and comprehend the influence our government can exert through its various policies in attempting to achieve industrial stability.

We look to the future with a confident hope that our educational institutions will measure up to their obligations to our country, and that the leaders of the future in the fields of education, finance, industry, government, agriculture and labor will bring to their tasks free, independent, dedicated minds devoted to the well-being of all the people. If we each succeed in our own field to measure up to this responsibility, it will all add up to a dynamic free society, one in which individual freedom will be used to guard and extend the freedom of the individual. From the University of North Carolina, serving a region where these problems are most complicated, American labor expects a correspondingly greater and more valuable contribution.

The Business and Business School Trained Executive in Government

By

JAMES E. WEBB

President, Republic Supply Company
Former Undersecretary of State
Former Director of the Bureau of the Budget

IT IS A HIGH HONOR to be back in my native State today to participate in this dedication of new facilities to the training of men and women for service to our nation and to the world. The University of North Carolina has a long tradition of reaching out to see the problems which must be faced by citizens and of building into the University the resources of faculty and training to keep its graduates ever marching forward. In the industrialization of the South, this Business School has had no small part to play. The liberal arts tradition of the whole University has combined with the research and teaching of the Business School to give a foundation for broader understanding and more creative leadership. This is what men like Dudley DeWitt Carroll, O. Max Gardner and the members of the Hanes Family, for whom these new facilities are named, have stood for and worked for; and by the power of their personal example, driven deep into the roots of our social and economic life. All North Carolina, indeed the nation knows with what beauty, and graciousness, and deep perception Mrs. O. Max Gardner has played her part in the events of the times. The tradition that surrounds the O. Max Gardner Hall is the richer because she is enfolded in it.

In the early days of our nation, government was largely a matter of exhortation, and political philosophy, and courts of law. Much of it was negative. Today, as we search the horizons of a world still new to us, and seek to build national strength and international partnership, there is a new requirement—that of effective administration of large action programs. This is the positive side of modern government. The university, and particularly the business school, must help to produce the skill to meet this requirement. Businessmen, who have sharpened and perfected this skill by experience and made it a habit of work, must enter government at a number of different levels in order to combine their special competence with other kinds of know-how.

A few days ago in the City of Boston, I walked down a street named for George Washington and I came to the Old South Meeting House. The inscription read: "Here were held the town meetings that ushered in the Revolution. Here Samuel Adams, James Otis and Joseph Warren exhorted. Here the men of Boston proved themselves independent, courageous, free men ready to raise issues which were to concern the liberty and happiness of millions yet unborn." Samuel Adams was the leader and the chief exhorter. In many ways he was the father of the Revolution. He was the political genius who understood emotions, prejudice, and the brilliant fire kindled by love of liberty. But the arguments for strong centers of executive and administrative power were lost on him. Harking back to the Town Meeting, he advocated a system of government by committee as the surest protection to individual liberty. His thesis was rejected. The framers of the Constitution considered stalemate and compromise in time of national crisis as paramount dangers. They decided that in our kind of nation it was necessary to fix responsibility for decision and action on one great national leader—the president of the United States. They adopted the doctrine of executive power and responsibility.

State governments have followed the national pattern and have developed real power in the office of the governor. Only from the bastion of a powerful office could Governor Gardner say, in 1930, "I am facing the gravest situation that has confronted North Carolina since the Civil War . . . I have set my face like flint against a special session . . . no power on earth could hold it in the bounds of reason and irreparable harm would inevitably come to the State." This is quoted from a letter to Mr. B. B. Gossett, February 1, 1930.

The doctrine of executive power and responsibility has from time to time been used, as Governor Gardner used it, as a brake on too hasty action. But that is only one use. More recently it has be-

come the handle by which to grasp the thorny problems of governmental administration. The executive budget, which has become
so essential to the effective operation of our political system, is an
outgrowth. The chief executive of state and nation is required to
submit to the representatives of the people in legislature and Congress for their approval at each session the whole program of activity, cost and taxation, which is proposed to implement policy
and meet public needs. It is this doctrine, evolved over the years,
which requires the chief executive in state and nation not only
faithfully to administer the laws of the land but to select and super-
vise subordinates through whom he must manage tremendous
undertakings of vast scope and complexity. The American doctrine
and practice of constitutional democracy has always been an evolv-
ing, developing, dynamic thing. Governmentally we have not
chained ourselves to the status quo. Our doctrine of executive power
and responsibility has developed, not as a challenge to the basic
concept of divided powers, but as a means of making that concept
work. The responsible government executive is the need of this
hour—an executive holding authority commensurate with responsibility, backed up by able and experienced subordinates, faithfully carrying out the policies and action programs enacted into
law, keeping adequate records of work done and results accomplished, making a full disclosure of all pertinent facts to the representatives of the people, and insisting that public debate and decision respond to organized facts rather than to organized prejudice.
Our democracy has produced better policy than it has administration. We are a little like the farmer who refused to attend a
demonstration of new methods, saying: "It's no use. I ain't farming
half as good now as I know how."

We are only half way through this century and yet numerous
empires have fallen; imperial systems have declined; two great
World Wars have unleashed vast destructive forces; and two im-
mense Revolutions—the Russian and the Chinese—have run a course
of extreme scope and intensity. International conspiracy has become the aggressive weapon of powerful dictatorships. The "Peace
Offensive" shows itself to be the "Offensive through the Peace
Issue." The world is permeated with uncertainty and the people

look to government for action. Policy must come first; action programs follow.

In the United States both policy and program are the result of public debate and political decision. They generally leave in their wake dissident minorities. Under these circumstances the efficient and businesslike execution of government action programs is of extreme importance. Unless these programs are carried out so effectively as to minimize questions of administrative competence, the adequacy of the policy is hard to judge. Our legislative representatives in this process of democracy must find a way to weed out the policy or program that is ineffective and to strengthen those that really get results. Our democracy has no sure and easy test by which to determine the public interest. But it will do a better job with the criteria we do have if we can raise our public debates to the policy level and get away from the personal recriminations that accompany questions of administrative competence.

The business community has a special responsibility because it is the largest reservoir of individuals experienced in large-scale operations. Administrative efficiency is hard to achieve and, in government, it is particularly difficult.

Several years ago the Comptroller General of the United States, the Honorable Lindsay C. Warren, undertook the leadership of a program to improve governmental administration through better accounting and record-keeping. He knew, from his long experience, that the fundamental relationships between the executive and legislative branches were strained and distorted by inability to find common meeting ground from which to observe the results of the policies and programs which had been enacted into law. At the start he knew he faced ten years of grinding work and he knew he could succeed only through persuasion, consent, cooperation and professional staff work. He joined with the Secretary of the Treasury and the Director of the Budget. He thoroughly reorganized the General Accounting Office; by the power of his personal leadership, he ended jurisdictional difficulties which had persisted for almost a hundred years. Without the vision and leadership of this hardheaded North Carolinian, trained in this University, a tremendous step forward would still be but a vision of the future. But it is important also to recognize that without the solid work and support of professionally trained accountants, businessmen and governmental administrators little could have been accomplished.

Where did Mr. Warren find these professional men? Certainly, some came from Chapel Hill. Others came from accounting and business. Still others were civil servants, grown gray in honorable service, or fresh with the youthful zest of a first major assignment. The nation needs many such men. The opportunity for service in this field is greater than any other that I know. It is fortunate indeed that North Carolina is stepping up its effort to meet such needs.

How many of us comprehend the magnitude and complexity of Government today? In 1952 there were 116,743 separate Government units in the United States. Since Korea, the United States Army has had to spend between twenty and thirty billions of dollars for every kind and description of equipment. Right now the Army is struggling with the problem of managing a troop program of one and one-half million young Americans scattered all over the world and requiring food, clothing, shelter, spiritual guidance, rotation, and training in almost every art—from electronics to hand-to-hand combat. This troop program covering one and one-half million men and this Army procurement program involving tens of billions of dollars, are but two of fifteen major administrative program entities of our modern Department of the Army. And this vast Department of the Army is but one of many large-scale organized efforts carried on by the Federal Government.

The Federal Research and Development Program is now running at something over two billions of dollars a year. It sets the pace for massive effort in universities and in industry which brings the annual total for the nation to some five billions of dollars. It has a profound impact on the future of every phase of our national life. The military part has heretofore been directed by the Research and Development Board of the Department of Defense. Under President Eisenhower's reorganization, this direction will pass to one man—an Assistant Secretary of Defense. If precedent is a guide, around this Assistant Secretary will be clustered a small group of able minds—some knowledgeable as to science, some knowledgeable as to military applications, and, most important, some knowledgeable in administration. Each of these men, looking at some specialized area of the responsibilities of this new office, must be able to think at the same time in terms of total responsibilities. Each project must produce results, and all must fit together. This new Assistant Secretary of Defense for Research and Development handling a program of $1.6 billion a year will be but one of ten new Assistant Secretaries needed to manage our military establishment. Each of these ten will have heavy responsibilities and need professional management assistance.

We have already invested twelve billions of dollars in the atomic energy field in a few brief years. The pattern for the transfer of the manufacture and development of atomic materials from the Federal government to private industry is now being worked out. Most likely the present Atomic Energy Commission will become some kind of regulatory agency and be relieved of its present large operations. But all this must be done by legislation, and our able and wise congressman from Chapel Hill, the Honorable Carl Durham, is going to have to wrestle in the Joint Committee with the problem of where power and responsibility are to come to rest. We can be certain that the first form cast up by the democratic process, even with the wisdom of a Carl Durham, will not be a perfect form. It will need a period in which administrators, and businessmen, and judicial-minded commissioners show up both the strengths and weaknesses of the new agency; these men must be articulate to convey the results of their efforts to the public and to Congress. This process of constant improvement of policy as a result of lessons learned by experience with administration is a whole new field for improving the democratic process.

Effective governmental administration must draw on universities for those graduates who have gone out into business and achieved success. They can and should assume governmental positions of great power and influence. President Gordon Gray followed this pattern and rendered farsighted and distinguished public service as Secretary of the Army as well as in other important positions. Around such men, who necessarily deal with problems of vast scope and complexity, must be clustered a central staff group of both generalists and specialists imbued with an understanding of every phase of the responsibility of the leader of the group. Down the line from this central group is that large number of men and women who are the organized team, who must be capable of sustained cooperation, and for whom there must be some systematic ordering of operations. With a Federal civilian employment of two and one-half million, and a military force of over three million, the organization of team work and the systematic ordering of operations requires the same kind of professional skill that has proven so effective in American business. The know-how of the Business School graduate is at a premium. And business itself must find a way to spare more of its ablest minds for government service—not just in top positions, but down the line as members of the organized team.

The Federal Government this year will spend a billion dollars for hospital care. This will require more than medical skill; it will require administrative skill. The organization of effort to collect more than sixty billions of dollars of tax levies in one year is a task for which the Business School may well train its most able students. In American business today the paper work, or red tape, is now occupying the full-time effort of some six million persons—ten percent of our working force. The percentage in government is higher, and the challenge to the Business School to produce the men who can streamline these procedures, who can utilize them for more effective accomplishment of work, is so great as to stagger the imagination.

The hard disciplines of economics, accounting, production, marketing, money and banking, corporate finance, personnel management and statistics are the training grounds for those who are required to make government more efficient. There is no easy road to this training. The political scientists are of a different discipline. It is to the new Business School and the new competence it generates that the nation must look. The dedication of these halls reflects an earnest hope that the challenge will be met.

Businessmen have organized their support through the North Carolina Business Foundation. Leaders like Robert Hanes, first President of the Foundation, and a distinguished representative of our country in Germany in its formative post-war period, have shown the way to progress through participation in Government and through partnership with the University. Men like Vice-President William D. Carmichael Jr., have given years of devotion to make this dedication possible. The University stands ready. Former President Frank Graham conceived this partnership as one, to use his words, of "opportunity for leadership in the economic, social and cultural building of a great State and region." At the inception of the Business Foundation, in 1947, he wrote me from Indonesia in these terms: "We have some great plans for a great University in the service of a great people in a time of great need. The University is the strategic frontier of North Carolina. North Carolina is the leader in the new and advancing South. The South is the new potential frontier of America. America has an economic and moral leadership which must not be lost in the complexities, confusions, tensions and human needs of this hour."

Long before 1947 the then Governor Gardner and President Frank Graham teamed up to bring into being the Consolidated University. To Governor Gardner, this was the most significant public service of his long and distinguished career. He loved this State and this University and was proud to have a part in making it ready for the partnership that is now coming into full fruition.

The University stands ready for another reason. Faculty and students are eager for the partnership.

And so today the bringing together of faculty, students, graduates and active businessmen, here in halls named Carroll, Gardner and Hanes will continue to expand this community thinking devoted to teaching and study, to research and investigation, to organized facts and to organized effort. In the tradition of this great University, under the leadership of President Gordon Gray, who personally knows the dependence of effective democracy on professional competence, driven on by the vigor of a new and younger Dean, Thomas H. Carroll, this Business School may be counted upon to flourish and fulfill its destiny to contribute substantially to a pool of creative leadership for a better world.

Responsibilities of and to Teachers: Our Unsung Heroes

By

THOMAS B. McCABE

President, Scott Paper Company
and Former Chairman, Board of Governors, Federal Reserve System

THESE NEW BUILDINGS add much to the architectural charm of the University. Their dedication marks the beginning of another significant epoch in the illustrious history of this great and progressive educational institution. In this magnificent setting, the prophetic words of Woodrow Wilson, as spoken to us on the campus of Swarthmore College, when I was an undergraduate, seem to echo in the distance—"You are here to enrich the world, . . . and you impoverish yourselves if you forget your errand."

These three new buildings which you have dedicated today are the monumental symbols of the "imagineering" of the university's leaders and scores associated with them in the university, in the alumni body, in industry and in the legislature. It is fitting at this dedication ceremony that you honor them as well as the many illustrious names in the university's history over the past century and a half and those in the School of Business Administration and its predecessor School of Commerce during the past three decades.

In speaking at Swarthmore College in June 1950, I said that "when I was in college there was a close and excellent relationship between the students and faculty and to us then the faculty heads were giants of intellectual power and standing. I will never forget the friendliness and inspiration of my teachers. They are my unsung heroes and they, rather than any other single remembrance of college, epitomize my love and devotion to my alma mater." Other than parents, there is no group of people who have greater influence on our sons and daughters in their more formative years —and thus on the future of our country—than the teachers throughout our educational system.

Today more people are getting educated than ever before. The number of students in high school has been increasing nine and one-half times as fast as the population of the United States and the number in colleges three and one-half times.

Said the cynic, "I could have made a better world than this." To which the sage replied, "That is why God put you here. Go do it." In spite of what the skeptics say, it is my conviction that the education the young people today are getting in our schools and colleges is better than it has ever been. I firmly believe that our educational system is now making the most significant contributions in all of its history to the preservation of the American way of life, its freedoms and our higher standards of living. Accordingly, I have titled this very informal statement: *Our Unsung Heroes.*

Beautiful college buildings and the delightful atmosphere surrounding them are to be admired, but even more so are the people in them because it is they who give the buildings life and vitality. Without the life-giving and spiritual qualities of a strong faculty, these buildings would be merely mounds of stone and mortar. It is a strong faculty, under wise leadership, that makes an educational institution.

Fortunately, North Carolina's School of Business Administration is richly endowed with the physical, social, intellectual and moral attributes which will serve to make its School of Business Administration a dynamic influence. A school of this character does not become dynamic through sheer force of numbers, but, rather, because of the philosophy of the faculty who guide it. This faculty must prepare our young people to go forth into the confusing world with humbleness of spirit, openness of mind, and an intense desire to make the world a better place than they found it.

Every progressive businessman today realizes that a growing and improving educational system is imperative to the successful operation of our complex economy. He realizes that education is a basic prerequisite for leadership. The schools and colleges must provide not only formal education; they must also instill in their students the desire to continue to educate themselves throughout their careers.

The role of education has broadened. The complexity of the

present day world requires more and more educated men and women who can deal with the problems that continually face them.

Even to the most short-sighted businessman, the need for young men thoroughly versed in business methods must surely be obvious. The entire new concept for our complex business world is based upon scientific approach, management methods, personnel policies, and the like. The guesswork is gone. The haphazard executive who snapped off decisions on a "by guess and by gosh" formula has been relegated to the ash heap with the sweatshop and other relics of early American business.

A young man just out of school—business or otherwise—cannot be measured for a vice-president's chair. Only through his willingness to indulge an appetite for learning is a young man worth anything to the business world. Modern business detects an appalling attitude of "the world owes me and my ornate diploma a living" in too many of the young men being interviewed for employment.

Many of the most interesting and promising young people in our organization today are veterans. They have lived a life full of responsibilities; some of them have travelled to the far corners of the world and have had a series of maturing and broadening experiences. Their knowledge and perception of world affairs and world problems is astounding. They combine idealism with impatience toward soft thinking. Their educational experience at North Carolina and other institutions has been added to their many other qualifications. Their potential contribution to business is tremendous.

They may be expected to revitalize one of the essential traditions of the American heritage—a love of adventure and opportunity and a willingness to incur risk in the pursuit of great aims. Part of the worldwide trend toward dependence on government instead of individual initiative has its roots in a philosophy of security. Our young people today know from their own experience that over-emphasis on security constitutes a false goal. There is no safe haven, no bomb shelter, that can protect the individual from the major hazards that are sweeping the world today. The only path to survival lies in facing difficulties and dealing with them squarely. This was the path our forefathers took when they carved out of the wilderness a civilization dedicated to freedom and liberty. This is the path our youth have followed to preserve and defend those freedoms. We need have little fear that they will try to escape their responsibilities by seeking security through isolationism.

The basic principles that the college gives to the student are cornerstones to his success. He requires professional knowledge because business requires it. He must be a many-faceted young man because such are the modern demands of business. He has to have a broad cultural background—a knowledge of the great ideas, philosophies and discoveries of the past and present—for the business leaders of the future will have to call upon reserves much deeper than those required of many of our present executives.

Education is not just the absorption of factual knowledge, but the development of the ability to think and to adjust to environment. This constitutes the basis for effective teamwork. Formal education is by no means an end in itself.

There will always be a place on the business scene for the talented man whose drive and personal ambition will propel him to the top even if he lacks the advantage of education. Such a man's qualifications are unique. For one thing, no instructor and no textbook have defined for him what can and cannot be done. His mind is not shackled by convention and precedent. Neither Henry Ford nor Walter Chrysler held academic degrees; yet both men added substantially to the 20th Century mechanical marvel. Such men educate themselves. They are rare.

There appears to be another factor in favor of such a man. Because he earns his place through personal ambition and application he senses that his only security rests within himself, not with a company or government. The country could use more men who recognize that security is in the man, not the job.

The foregoing statements are meant in no way to minimize the role of the school or the educator, only to reflect an observation that education, in the final analysis, is subjective. The academic atmosphere is wasted if the individual refuses to breath deeply. It is also dissipated if it does not bring a proper perspective. The law school does not turn out judges, and the business school does not turn out Chairmen of the Board. For, important as the school or university is, it can only start a man out. The rest is partly up to the individual and partly up to his employer.

Despite the great increase in the number of trained and educated men coming to work in American business, there is still a great shortage of men who can take positions of business leadership. All of the expansion in our educational system and all of its formal instruction cannot supply us with enough leaders for an expanding economy unless education continues long after the diploma has turned yellow with age. The mission of formal education is to give our young people the background, the intellectual curiosity and the tools of learning that will enable them to seize the opportunities that come to them after they leave school. And we in business must see to it that these opportunities are preserved by keeping our economy strong, competitive, free and dynamic.

The educational institution's task never ends. It must keep on educating not just its students, undergraduate and graduate, but its alumni and the community as a whole.

One of the most important tasks of the business school is to help companies realize that their future depends on the development of the talent in their plants and offices. Executive development is a responsibility of special note. There is always going to be a shortage of such talent, and it would be tragic to waste it. University programs which are carefully designed may contribute significantly to an effective over-all attack on this problem.

But let us return to this university and its relationship with business. Your past 30 years have been phenomenal in their results. Your high standards and excellent faculty have placed you in the select circle of fine business schools.

Business recognizes that there must be a reciprocal responsibility incumbent upon business to assist the institutions who supply management manpower. If the American educational institutions are to be called upon to provide this basic training for business, then business itself must surely assume a friendly, cooperative and appreciative attitude toward those who form the cadre for the training program. The firm recognition that industry must join hands with educators has yet to permeate all business. To some extent, this reflects a carry-over of the attitude prevalent at the turn of the century when business felt it had fulfilled its responsibility merely by providing jobs. Fortunately for the country, disciples of this unrealistic religion are being replaced by men with conscience, men who understand the intimate association of business and the many publics, including education.

What, then, can and must business do to draw itself nearer to the world of education?

First, I believe the marriage of theory and practice is ideal; business can supply the latter in almost limitless quantities. Just as business should be charged with the need for getting its men into the schools where they can add further chapters to the textbooks, educators should be cautioned not to guard their teaching prerogatives so closely that they shut out a valuable source of help and guidance. Business and schools each have volumes for the other; each must constantly make overtures to see that the two forces are united.

Further, it is recommended—indeed, urged—that there be greater use of the so-called field trip, in which the student moves from the confines of the school to the busy industrial plant. No doubt we could rationalize to a degree our failure to show all America the inside of an industrial operation, but what a pathetic commentary on both school and industry when in so many cases the business student knows no more about industry than he has read on the pages of a text. A cordial invitation is extended to the teaching fraternity to visit and consult with industry, to see principles and theories tried before the bar of practical application. Visitations by members of faculties would do much to expedite the uninhibited exchange of ideas between school and industry.

The business of today is a living part of the community. Most businessmen recognize their duty and responsibility to their community. But it is surprising how many of them can think of no way in which they can perform the service they recognize as part of their job.

The business school can contribute to the development of participation by businessmen in local and national affairs. It can even help to develop the talents of businessmen in community responsibility to the point where some of them, like Dean David, President Gray and others, put in some time in the service of their government.

In the thirty year life of this business school at the University of North Carolina, a good many changes have taken place, changes which have had their effect on all of us. In those three decades, the responsibility for the leadership of all free nations has come to the United States. We have outgrown the isolationism that existed during the first 150 years of the history of this University. We grow daily in our responsibility to friendly nations. Startling changes in industry have created brand new products, improved methods, dramatic techniques. Social changes in the business world have not been so startling, perhaps, but they have contributed beyond measure to our mature economic system in which the dignity of man is coming to be as treasured as a production record.

Many of you who have grown up with this business school have recognized its changes—not only in its physical dimensions and number of students, but in the modern teaching methods which have evolved. You may not have recognized the changes as they occurred, but you see them clearly in retrospect. That is the illusory character of change.

There will always be a premium on flexibility in our lives, because the only thing unchanging in this world is the certainty of change itself. No school, no business, no individual can refuse to conform to change. Even more, we must guide the change, for change means new opportunities. The static college damages its reputation and jeopardizes the potential of its students. The immutable businessman quickly falls as the pace set by his competitors, who seize the commercial advantages of change, overwhelms him. And the rugged individual who bases his sorry life on the "good enough for father" principle either lives in a traumatic nightmare or serves absolutely no place in society. Change for all of us must be more than a thing passively tolerated. It must be a challenge accepted in the tradition of a duel. It will always be an effective weapon in the hand of the man who meets it halfway.

Some of the greatest changes in the past generation have taken place in the business arena. Even the reputation of business itself has passed through several phases. When World War II broke out in Europe, the standing of the American businessman with the public was still near the low point it had reached during the depression.

The war made it urgently necessary to shift the entire emphasis of the American economy from civilian to military output. And in an economy still concerned with recovery from history's greatest depression, we found ourselves faced with the problem of vastly expanding our production. It was necessary also to deal with the change in psychology occasioned by the arrival of a new force in the economy. The depression had given rise to a philosophy of defeatism. The American economy, it was said, had passed maturity and reached a point of stagnation. Many believed that technology had reached its final stage of achievement and that the era of economic growth and progress had come to a close. The scientist distrusted the businessman, the businessman distrusted the government, and the government looked upon the businessman as a combined villain and scapegoat.

The need for action, however, helped to bring the dissident elements of American leadership together. The businessman suddenly found that the entire war program revolved about him. For when great production deeds had to be accomplished, the nation turned to business.

It appears perfectly safe to contend that American business grew up during World War II. We found that the depression had not killed enterprise, invention, or scientific and technological progress. We reaffirmed our belief in the enormous resilience and flexibility of a free and competitive economy and in its prodigious capacity. We emerged from the war with renewed confidence not only in our economic system but in our own capabilities. The businessman had learned many lessons during the depression and the war, and he emerged more confident and vastly more experienced.

In November, 1952, with the assistance of the South, the American people elected a new administration, one that did not seek to avail itself of the services of the business community on the one hand and castigate it for political advantage on the other. The new administration has been inaccurately characterized as a "Business" administration. While it includes many businessmen, it also includes a former labor leader, many educators, several former state governors, career diplomats, journalists, economists and others. It is an administration that seeks to find the best talent in all fields.

But if the new administration is not a "Business" administration, it is one in which the businessman is taking more leadership and more responsibility. The business community must justify the confidence that has been placed in the businessman after years of distrust and scorn. And, like the rest of the community, the business community must have patience with our new leaders. Many of the new men in Washington are still unfamiliar with the devious and often cruel ways of government. They are still learning their new jobs and at the same time carrying out the operation of the world's most important government in an unusually critical time.

Of course, the administration must expect criticism and political attacks. Irresponsibility seems to be a common commodity. Some business groups still feel that they must over-plead their case. It is evident that more public responsibility, more effective citizenship, and better leadership are required. *There* is a job for education.

Fortunately, some groups are taking responsible positions and a realistic view of what can be accomplished in today's world as, for example, The Committee for Economic Development, with which Secretary of the Treasury Humphrey, his Under Secretary, Marion Folsom, and Under Secretary of Commerce Walter Williams were so closely identified. Some people in Congress and in business still feel that inflationary fiscal policies should be continued but the CED has objectively urged against cutting taxes until we can balance the budget. While some would reverse the gains we have made toward ensuring our national security, the CED is urging that we strive for broader trade, greater economic and political collaboration between nations, and pursuit of the objectives of mutual security. Other organizations are also taking this constructive position.

We need more thinking of this sort, and we need more patience with the men who hold the fate of the entire free world in their hands. The public needs more education so that it will not make an emotional response to the irresponsible men who are seeking to thwart the development of rational policies for the benefit of the public as a whole. And since business has now identified itself with capable leadership, it has assumed at least part of the burden of seeing to it that the education of the public becomes a fact. Business can be of unlimited service in this direction.

Not the least of the services business can and must render is the expenditure of money in the area of higher education. If we are to continue the intellectual growth of the nation and the expansion of education that make our economic and social gains possible, we must open new sources for the financing of our educational system and for the higher education of more of our talented young people.

One of the best financial sources is American business, which has so greatly benefited from the advance of education. Business, within the limits established by law and sound business practice, can do more than provide grants for research in projects of direct interest to itself. The recent court decision of Superior Court Judge Alfred A. Stein of New Jersey "that corporations have both a valid right and a solemn duty to make financial contributions to educational institutions"—in the words of the *New York Times*—is of interest. Corporations can also help to finance the even more difficult and important project of developing the leaders of to-morrow. In this new role, business must in no way interfere with academic freedom, for it is not its prerogative to dictate what shall be taught and how.

It appears to me that the Business Foundation of North Carolina exemplifies much of what I am advocating. I commend its action.

It was earlier stated that free interchange between school and business creates a meeting ground where each can inspect at close range the ideas and techniques of the other. Never before has the opportunity been more provocative. Business's reputation stands at a new high. Its larder of know-how has been filled by government service; its judgment has been mellowed by the depression; and its abilities have been sharpened by the remarkable post-war conversion. In every sense, the American businessman is ready to instruct the next generation of executives, and what's more, he sincerely wants to do so.

The schools themselves can contribute more than ever before to the goal of better business management, for they have reached mature judgment in what constitutes able administration in business. They are stripping courses of the traditional frills and they are eliminating the misconceptions about industry that prevailed even among the educated. Further, they can see the ills that still plague certain elements of business, and they can prescribe, perhaps more objectively than management itself, the cures for these latent sicknesses.

Business and the schools depend on each other. Both will suffer, later if not right now, if they do not commit themselves to joint action and study. I have become so convinced of this fact that I want to make the following offer. Scott Paper Company would like very much to invite a member of the faculty of the School of Business Administration at Chapel Hill to join the company for a calendar year, or an academic year, as a full member of the organization. Suitable salary arrangements and other allowances would be made so that the faculty member would not suffer monetarily; in fact, we would hope to make the leave of absence work to his economic advantage. I can think of very few instances that have worked to the financial advantage of teachers in our colleges and universities. They are without doubt the most underpaid people for what they contribute of any element in our society.

I recommend that a committee be formed, composed of representatives of the University of North Carolina and Scott Paper Company, to select such a man. He would be chosen by virtue of his interest in business and his demonstrated abilities as an educator. We will offer to the faculty member chosen to work with the company a program in which not only will he learn as much of practical business as we can collectively teach him, but he will make substantial contributions to our business based on his knowledge of the science of management.

In return, the company will make available, at no cost to the University, men of considerable experience in Scott operations to appear as guest lecturers as often as is reasonably desirable. In this way, the exchange will be complete and meaningful. The dean and others of his staff can determine among themselves in what ways and to what extent these men will be utilized to draw the fullest good from their business background.

In making this suggestion, the company hopes in some small way to open up a two-way system between school and business and collect for each the rewards of bilateral study and exposure. We sincerely hope that arrangements for this plan will be possible between this fine university and our company.

This visit to one of the most progressive institutions in the progressive South has been a deep and rewarding experience. May I express my personal salutation to all of you whose lives are devoted to the most rewarding of all vocations—the instruction of the youth. *You are the Unsung Heroes.*

The dedicated men and women of this educational center have renewed my faith in what lies ahead for the young men and women whose heritage will be just what *we* choose to make it. Business and education have the exciting opportunity to be partners in preparing this heritage. For each, there is the prospect of tremendous gratification in achievement; and for each, the sober responsibility of errorless judgment. The enlightened businessman and the educator with vision can and will form an alliance which will carry our great country to ever greater heights.

APPENDICES

I.

EXCERPTS FROM DEDICATORY GREETINGS

ARCHIBALD T. FORT, *President, Beta Gamma Sigma,*
University of North Carolina

THIS IS A DAY of great importance in North Carolina, for today
three new buildings are being dedicated to this university and to
the School of Business Administration. These three buildings,
Gardner, Hanes and Carroll Halls . . . are the newest on the campus of the oldest state university. These buildings are a valuable
addition to the campus itself; a notable achievement in 158 years
of progress since 1795 when the total university plant consisted of
a single unimposing building surrounded by a virgin forest.

And yet in spite of their newness, these buildings are close to
the heart and hub of university life. They stand a stone's throw
from the first building erected on this campus whose cornerstone
was laid in 1793. They are set in the midst of a physical plant of
ivy-covered buildings, and mark finally the completion of the original plans of campus development. . . .

Coupled with these new buildings, the administration and faculty of the School of Business Administration are today the largest
and the most competent that it has ever had. The administration is
optimistic and progressive. It is efficient and helpful; it gives us
as students confidence that we are being guided not only academically, but in other ways, toward becoming useful, satisfied
citizens of our community life.

The faculty is composed of men of experience and insight; men
who love to study and to teach; men who selflessly direct their lives
for the welfare of their school and the students whom they teach;
men who contribute widely to the world of business and government; whose writings have proven their merit and whose standing
among the educators in their respective fields has been recognized
time and time again by their receiving fellowships and other grants
and their election to offices of regional and national importance.

We as students rely tremendously upon this school. It is here that we will get some of the most important training in all our lives. . . .

Here we have great opportunities for developing ourselves for positions of responsibility in private business and government, but we need your help. We ask you to encourage students with creative minds, to guide us all as we develop habits of thought and action, to teach, to advise and to lead.

With enthusiasm, with open minds, and with hearts full of appreciation to the people of this state, the students join with others who are among the first to make use of these new buildings. In the coming years they shall be of immeasurable benefit to us all. . . .

WILLIAM WELLS, *Professor of English and*
Chairman of the General Faculty of the University

THE GENERAL FACULTY welcomes the addition of these three splendid buildings to the physical plant of the University. Their beauty and present use speak eloquently for them; what they symbolize has an even greater eloquence: for over three decades integrity in learning and in teaching has been the mark of the . . . school.

R. ARTHUR SPAUGH, *President, Alumni Association of the*
University of North Carolina

CAROLINA ALUMNI, WHEREVER they may be, almost 50,000 of them, are joined in extending hearty congratulations to our Alma Mater, on the completion, and now the presentation of these magnificent buildings of the School of Business Administration. The names Carroll, Gardner, and Hanes, will themselves be an inspiration to all who enter here. . . .

In the fastest moving world of all times business finds itself facing new situations constantly. Never before has its need for new workable ideas been so imperative. . . . Never before has the time for the capacity to think and plan intelligently in business been so great. Here in Chapel Hill with these increased facilities, the improved training of the minds of the students in this school should do much towards filling this need for new ideas.

ARTHUR R. WEIMER, *President, American Association of Collegiate Schools of Business*

IT IS A GREAT PLEASURE on behalf of the American Association of Collegiate Schools of Business to congratulate the University of North Carolina on these splendid new buildings designed to serve the growing educational needs in business administration. . .

The Association is pleased to see the significance accorded the field of business administration by the University as evidenced by these fine new facilities for study, teaching, research and service to the business community.

While men are always more important than materials, faculty members more important than buildings, both are needed in sound proportions to do an effective job. I know from my own experience that new buildings stimulate faculty members and students to better efforts; they make for greater efficiency; they serve as symbols of progress and past achievement. . .

In many respects the study of business administration is still in its pioneering stage. We feel certain that the University of North Carolina will make great contributions to the further development of this dynamic area of study. I predict that in a few decades such progress will be made that even these fine buildings will be inadequate to meet your requirements in the field of professional education for business.

CALVIN B. HOOVER, *President, American Economic Association*

IT IS A PARTICULAR pleasure to represent the American Economic Association at the dedication of Dudley DeWitt Carroll Hall, O. Max Gardner Hall and Hanes Hall with their superb new facilities for research and instruction in business administration and economics. . . .

. . . These magnificent facilities belong to us, the citizens of North Carolina, for service in the cause of advancing knowledge for all the world. We can feel that in this dedication North Carolina is taking a significant step forward. We of the faculty of Duke University do not forget that the University of North Carolina is our university, too. We have the same pride in the improvement of its facilities as do all our neighbors in the whole state.

Speaking for the American Economic Association, we are proud that these facilities are now available for the use of faculty and students in the field of economics and business administration at a time when the tasks for us in these related fields are greater and more difficult than ever before. The pure and applied science of the physicist, the chemist, the biologist and the engineer, developed in the United States as in no other country in the whole world, afford us the basis for a standard of living for our people which is likewise unequalled elsewhere. Yet placing this vast fund of scientific and engineering knowledge at the service of the people of the United States depends as well upon the industrial entrepreneur, the banker, the business manager, the accountant and the salesman.

Under present circumstances, specialists in all these fields require the same high quality of training as do scientists and engineers. It is the function of the economist to analyze the complex operations of our economic organism and, upon the basis of this analysis, to give the kind of advice to industry, agriculture, labor, and government which should enable us to prevent financial and economic crises from wrecking our economic system. To myself and to the thousands of my colleagues of the American Economic Association the dedication of these facilities gives the same deep satisfaction that comes to our brethren of the physical sciences when a great new laboratory is built and opened for use. The training of both future economists and executive personnel for commerce and industry will be greatly furthered by the facilities provided in this new building complex. We feel a real sense of satisfaction since because of this dedication the economists of the University of North Carolina have a better opportunity to help all of us economists fulfill our obligations to society.

Our very best wishes and our highest expectations will always be with our friends of the School of Business Administration in their occupancy and utilization of these halls.

BENJAMIN U. RATCHFORD, *President, Southern Economic Association*

IT IS A HIGH HONOR and a great pleasure for me to join with you today in the dedication of these magnificent new facilities of the School of Business Administration. . . .

This university has been most closely identified with the Southern Economic Association since that association was organized some twenty-five years ago. The faculty members of this school have participated in every major activity of the association and two of your distinguished members—Professor Woosley and Professor Schwenning—have served with high credit as its president. Some seventeen years ago, on this campus, this university and the association joined hands to establish the *Southern Economic Journal,* a publication which since then has won for itself a place of high esteem and prestige among the learned journals of this country and of the world. Your university has been most generous in its support of the *Journal* and much of the credit for its illustrious record must go to your Professor Schwenning who, almost continuously from its beginning, has served with outstanding loyalty and efficiency as its managing editor. He has thereby built a lasting monument for himself and for his university.

To me these beautiful new buildings are symbolic in several respects. They are symbolic, first, of a higher and rising level of income and economic well-being in the South. Only a few short years ago no educational institution in the whole Southland, whether public or private, could have afforded such elegant facilities. They are symbolic, secondly, of the growing importance of economics, industry, commerce and finance in the developing economy of the South. Thirdly, they are symbolic of public recognition of the great need for trained and educated leadership in these fields. Finally, they are symbolic of the close interrelationship and interdependence of theoretical economics and the applied arts of business administration, which are here combined into one great school. Theoretical economics can analyze, explain, and appraise the significance of broad economic developments and provide a sound basis for a program of economic development, but it cannot translate its findings into workable programs for the individual firm or industry. In the same way, business administration can aid the businessman in numerous ways to plan his activities, to do his job more efficiently, and to avoid mistakes, but it must depend upon economics to indicate the broad lines of development and the fields of activity which should be emphasized. Here in one school those two disciplines are brought together so that they can integrate their work and supplement each other. The opportunities which they have for constructive co-operation in promoting economic development are almost unlimited. We shall follow your work with the keenest interest and with the most cordial wishes for success.

ROBERT M. HANES, *Charter Member and First President, Business Foundation of North Carolina*

I AM HONORED TO REPRESENT the Business Foundation of North Carolina on the occasion of the dedication of these wonderful new buildings of the School of Business Administration.

As we view these splendid facilities, we are moved by strong feelings of achievement and inspiration. In physical terms the achievement, as you can see, is measurably great. The university has long wanted and needed these halls. The School of Business Administration, and its antecedent, the School of Commerce, has been a fast-growing and invaluable part of the university since 1919. Its needs have been most acute in the past decade. No group has been more aware of this situation than the Business Foundation, and, beginning with its establishment in 1946, the Foundation has sought steadily to bring about an expansion of the facilities of the business school. The General Assembly of North Carolina should be congratulated for its recognition of the need for these buildings, and for its wise action in appropriating funds to provide them. Here, then, is a substantial achievement for the university, for the state, for the Foundation, and for the people of North Carolina. From this, all of us who are interested in the economic soundness of North Carolina and the progress of our state can draw immeasurable inspiration.

The School of Business Administration and the Business Foundation represent a partnership of business and education which recognizes the needs, the challenges, and the potentialities of North Carolina's economy. This is a working partnership which provides a means of achieving for this state a dynamic economy, second to none. The greatest of our universities have attained their excellence because of private support supplementing public grants. The business community of North Carolina is happy and proud because of the part it plays in the building of a great School of Business Administration at our university.

In these buildings will be taught and trained our business leaders of the years to come, who will be, I am confident, prepared and determined to lift this state and its business life to higher peaks of accomplishment than was possible by the preceding generations of businessmen in the state who had no such opportunity for learning and research.

The university, the Business Foundation, and the legislature, have all shown that they realize that business progress enriches the whole people. Let us recognize that it must never be our purpose simply to teach students to achieve business success. A curriculum designed for such purpose would make a school of business administration no more than a trade school. We must, instead, set a goal of a full and fair economy which will bring enrichment to all the people of North Carolina through providing a higher standard of living, a more stable income, and a fuller development of our abundant resources, especially our human resources. We must inspire the students with high ideals and a conscientious spirit of service which will guide them in their business life and strengthen them in their citizenship.

We can well recall the words of Woodrow Wilson to a student group: "You are not here merely to prepare to make a living; you are here to enable the world to live more amply, with a greater vision and the finer spirit of hope and achievement. You are here to enrich the world, not yourselves alone, and you will impoverish yourselves if you forget your errand."

II.

RESPONSE TO DEDICATORY GREETINGS

THOMAS H. CARROLL, *Dean, School of Business*
Administration, University of North Carolina

THIS IS, I BELIEVE, a justifiably proud moment for me as representative of my colleagues of the faculty of the School of Business Administration, including the Department of Economics. We appreciate tremendously the expressions of confidence and good will conveyed in these splendid messages presented to us on behalf of a number of the "publics" which this school serves.

We recognize clearly that it is not physical surroundings alone which make a great school, college or university. The "core" element, to use a term common in modern educational parlance at all levels, is people. But we must hasten to recognize also that effective people—students and faculty—in a school such as ours are enabled to increase their productivity when fine physical facilities are made available to them. We now have such facilities.

We are grateful to the Board of Trustees for recognizing the need for these facilities when the presentation was made to them several years ago by the administrative officers of the predecessor School of Commerce and of the university. We are grateful to the General Assembly of the State of North Carolina, and thus to the people of the state, for appropriating the necessary funds. We believe that those funds have been used wisely as well as economically. This is one of the very unusual building projects of modern times which cost substantially less than either the original appropriation or the contractors' estimates.

We express our thanks for the untiring efforts of the members of our Faculty Committee on Building and Equipment of which Professor Dudley J. Cowden served as chairman. To Mrs. Dudley J. Cowden we are deeply indebted for countless hours of voluntary assistance which have made our surroundings pleasant as well as useful.

With utmost sincerity and complete humility we rededicate

ourselves as we dedicate these buildings which constitute our splendid new home. We rededicate ourselves to the threefold task of effective class and seminar teaching, of creating new knowledge in our inherently dynamic fields through research, and of service to the state, region, nation and the world.

The newest and one of the most significant of our services which will be added to our extension activities, conferences and institutes is The Executive Program which is now being developed by a group of our faculty under the leadership of Professor Willard J. Graham. A detailed announcement of this program will be issued shortly. The schedule and curriculum of The Executive Program have been especially designed to serve effectively the top executive development needs of business and industry within the state and the southeastern region.

We are happy to announce that, as a result of the financial underwriting by the Business Foundation, we will conduct this summer a three week Workshop in Economic Education for about seventy public school teachers and supervisors under the joint sponsorship and management of the Schools of Education and Business Administration and with the cooperation of the Joint Council for Economic Education. The program represents a recognition of a major deficiency in our total educational effort and an attempt to meet it in part at a jugular point. Dr. Milton Heath, professor of economics, will be academic director of this important project.

In the words of one of this country's most able business statesmen, Frank W. Abrams, board chairman of the Standard Oil Company (New Jersey); "It is easy to be suspicious of the aims and purposes of people you do not know. The foundation of good human relationships must be faith . . ." If we are to teach economics and business effectively we believe we must keep in touch with economic and business affairs, and the men and women who determine economic and business policy. In his inaugural address as President of Columbia University, Dwight D. Eisenhower expressed a philosophy which we accept: "The school that enjoys a partnership with manufacturing industries and labor unions and mercantile establishments of its community is a better and more productive school in consequence of its non-academic associations. Its influence permeates the entire community and is multiplied many times over while the school itself, energized by the challenges and dynamism of community life, grows and broadens with each problem it helps surmount."

At the same time we recognize our responsibility for constructive criticism, for the development of new theory. As I have stated elsewhere: "The increasing public aspects of private business and the increasing need for managing economic forces point forcefully to a community of interest between academicians and managers. Change in the area of management could and should result more typically from work initiated by the academic mind and developed with the cooperation of policy-makers. Such results cannot be reasonably expected, however, if men in academic life are proceeding on unfounded hunches or outdated facts about the administrative world." If we are to meet this need, we shall have to provide increased travel funds for field research in economics and business administration.

Progress and change are not synonymous. It is, however, difficult to conceive of progress without some change. To quote Abrams again: ". . . Business attitudes and practices change, but they sometimes change slowly." Educators cannot effect the changes but they can and should have an important role in suggesting possible avenues for constructive changes.

Finally, we recognize that our central interest is the student, be he undergraduate, graduate, business executive or economic policy-maker. We trust that our efforts in research and service as well as in teaching will be constantly directed toward his development not as an over-specialized technician in any sense but as a whole man—a human being, a citizen, and a responsible man of business and economic affairs. Our objective as a faculty in helping to develop our students is well-expressed in the following prayer by a famous general:

"Build me a son, O Lord, who will be strong enough to know when he is weak, and brave enough to face himself when he is afraid; one who will be proud and unbending in honest defeat, and humble and gentle in victory.

"Build me a son whose wishbone will not be where his backbone should be; a son who will know Thee—and that to know himself is the foundation stone of knowledge.

"Lead him, I pray, not in the path of ease and comfort, but under the stress and spur of difficulties and challenge. Here let him learn to stand up in the storm; here let him learn compassion for those who fail.

"Build me a son whose heart will be clear, whose goal will be high; a son who will master himself before he seeks to master other men; one who will learn to laugh, yet never forget how to weep; one who will reach into the future, yet never forget the past.

"And after all these things are his, *add,* I pray, enough of a sense of humor, so that he may always be serious, yet never take himself too seriously. Give him humility, so that he may always remember the simplicity of true greatness, the open mind of true wisdom, the meekness of true strength.

"Then I, his father, will dare to whisper, 'I have not lived in vain.' "

III.

PRESENTATION OF CARROLL PORTRAIT

REMARKS BY CHANCELLOR ROBERT B. HOUSE
UNIVERSITY OF NORTH CAROLINA AT CHAPEL HILL
At
Unveiling of Portrait of Dudley DeWitt Carroll
Professor of Economics
And
Dean Emeritus of The School of Commerce
University of North Carolina

I WANT TO EXPRESS my delight that this group of buildings corre-
spond symmetrically to the group on the other side of the campus.
I wish to emphasize the symbolism in the situation. Carroll Hall
looks to Manning Hall, the home of law and justice. Gardner Hall
looks to Murphy Hall, the home of the languages, the classics,
and the drama. Hanes Hall looks to Saunders Hall, the home of
history and the social sciences. Beyond is Lenoir Hall where the
students dine. The moral of this symbolism is that unless businessmen ever look to law and justice and pass through the grounds of
a liberal arts education they are likely not to eat.

Dean Dudley Carroll, of the School of Commerce, who could
at any time have assumed the role of the Dean of the College of
Arts and Sciences, personifies this spirit of liberal education as a
foundation for business.

The presidents of the University of North Carolina as a rule
stay in office longer than is usual in the country. I think it is
remarkable that Professor Carroll served as dean with three university presidents. Edward Kidder Graham bought him here and
started him on his distinguished career. Harry Woodburn Chase
and Frank Porter Graham found him their loyal and effective
administrative colleague. It was largely as a result of his enthusiasm and willing cooperation that this physical expansion and
the careful selection and appointment of his successor as dean
took form in the administration of Gordon Gray.

Not only in the portrait and in Carroll Hall and in the School of Business Administration, but in the warp and woof of the entire University, Dudley Carroll's life and service are woven. I am glad to testify that he never shirked his responsibility to a single student for his personal comfort. During the summer when most of his colleagues were on vacation he was searching to see if students were worthy to come into the school. During Christmas, when others were celebrating, he was searching to see if students were worthy to return to his school. He never shirked upholding a standard for the sake of temporary pleasant relations with a student. This made him an unlikely candidate for any current popularity ballot; but the remarkable thing is that students, when they had gone out into the business world, came back to express affection and gratitude for his teaching.

It is said that the monument of Sir Christopher Wrenn in London bears the inscription, "If you wish to see the monument of me, look about you." All we have to do, to see in addition to this portrait the lasting features of Dudley DeWitt Carroll, is to look about us, in this building, in the School of Business Administration, in the entire university and in the state and nation. How blessed we are to have present with us the values of great teachers for a long time. There is present today not simply one of Dean Carroll's early teachers but, his first teacher, Mrs. Taylor of Danbury. Dudley DeWitt Carroll III is also present. I am going to ask him to come to the platform and unveil the portrait of his grandfather.

www.ingramcontent.com/pod-product-compliance
Lightning Source LLC
Chambersburg PA
CBHW021606210326

41599CB00010B/621